Weekly Reader Books presents

What to do
when your mom or dad says...
"WHAT SHOULD YOU SAY, DEAR?"

By
JOY WILT BERRY

Living Skills Press
Fallbrook, California

Weekly Reader Books offers several exciting
card and activity programs. For information,
write to WEEKLY READER BOOKS, P.O. Box 16636,
Columbus, Ohio 43216.

Dear Parents:

"WHAT SHOULD YOU SAY, DEAR?" Have you ever said this to your children and had them reply, "I don't know."

This issue is a matter of etiquette. Etiquette is not just an optional part of everyday living. In situations involving relationships, etiquette is essential. It is the guideline that shows us how to act in pleasing and acceptable ways, and it tells us how to be gracious around other people. Sound etiquette is based on three very important principles:

Do unto others as you would have them do unto you. Every one of us has a deep need to be treated with kindness and respect. If we hope to receive kindness and respect from other people, we must treat them with the same. Centered in this truth is the balance between "what's good for me" and "what's good for you," a balance which is necessary for the survival and growth of any human relationship.

Beauty is as beauty does. This means that our personal beauty depends on our behavior rather than on our physical appearance. In other words, it is how we act rather than how we appear which makes us ugly, or beautiful. No matter what we look like, crude behavior can make us ugly, while gracious behavior can make us beautiful in a very special way.

A thing of beauty is a joy forever! Think about it. When you are around something that is ugly, you probably feel sad and depressed. On the other hand, when you are around something that is beautiful, you probably feel inspired and happy.

It is the same way with people. Being around a person who is ugly because of crude behavior is often sad and depressing. However, being around a person who is beautiful because of gracious behavior is often inspiring and uplifting. Generally speaking, people do not want to be around a person who makes them feel depressed. Instead, they want to be around someone who makes them feel good.

If we are gracious, others will desire rather than resist our companionship. This is important as all of us are social beings.

Your children come into the world as social beings possessing specific social needs. Accompanying these needs are your children's innate abilities to get their needs met, but these abilities are undeveloped. One of your jobs as parents is to facilitate the development of these abilities. You can accomplish this by doing these things:

1. Help your children observe and evaluate their own behavior as it relates to others.
2. Bring your children into a basic understanding of the three principles mentioned above.
3. Help your children clarify social expectations.
4. Expose your children to guidelines which can enable them to meet valid social expectations.

This book can help you achieve these things. If you will use it systematically as part of a continuing program or as a resource to be used whenever the need for it arises, you and your children will experience some very positive results.

With your help, your children will have less and less need to have you say, **"WHAT SHOULD YOU SAY, DEAR?"** and will behave and respond to social situations graciously.

Sincerely,

Joy Wilt Berry

4

Has your mother or father ever said to you...

WHAT SHOULD YOU SAY, DEAR?

HELLO.

When your mom or dad says, "What should you say, dear?" do you ever wonder...

If any of this sounds familiar to you, you're going to **love** this book.

Because it will tell you all about introductions and how to handle them.

GRACIOUS INTRODUCTIONS

Introducing Yourself to a Person You Don't Know

Whenever you meet someone you don't know, you can be gracious by doing these things:

• Greet the person with a pleasant "Hello!"

• Tell the person your name.

• Ask the person what his or her name is.

Introducing People You Know to Each Other

If, while you are with a friend, you see someone you know, you can be gracious by acknowledging the person and introducing your friends to each other.

Whenever you want to introduce one person to another, you can be gracious by doing these things:

1. Address the person you are with. This means, look at the person and say his or her name. (Use the name for the person you usually use. In this case, you would say "Aunt Betty" rather than "Mrs. Smith.")

8

2. Tell the person you are with who the other person is, how you know each other, and what your friend's name is. (Use the name the other person is to use.)

If you forget a person's name, say something like...

3. Address the other person. This means, look at the person and say his or her name, using the name for the person you usually use.

4. Tell the other person about the person you are with. Tell how you know this person and what his or her name is. Use the name the other person is to use. For example, if it is your Aunt Betty, say. . .

Being Introduced to Someone

You can be gracious when you are being introduced by doing these things:

1. Look the person you are being introduced to in the eyes. After the person has been introduced, acknowledge the person by saying something, like "Hello, *(the person's name)*, I'm glad to meet you."

2. Shake the person's hand if it is held out for you to shake. If you like, you can be the first to start a handshake by holding out your hand.

Here are some things you need to know when you are being introduced to someone:

• If the person who is introducing you cannot remember your name, tell what it is in a kind way.

• If you are being introduced to someone who is standing up, you should try to stand up, too. Then you should not sit down until the others sit down.

After the Introduction

When you have been introduced to someone and your conversation is ended, you may want to say. . .

The most important thing to remember—

• when you introduce yourself to a person you don't know, or

• when you introduce people you know to each other, or

• when you are being introduced to another person,

is to TREAT OTHER PEOPLE THE WAY YOU WANT TO BE TREATED. If you follow this guideline, you will usually end up doing the right thing.

GRACIOUS CONVERSATIONS

Starting Conversations

If the other person does not start the conversation, you can begin it graciously by doing one of these two things:

- Give the person a sincere compliment. Be sure, however, that whatever you say is honest.

- Ask the person some questions like, "Where do you work?", "Where do you live?", "What are some of the things you like to do?"

Having a Conversation

You can carry on a gracious conversation by doing these six things:

1. Remember that a good conversation is an exchange, with both people doing some of the talking and some of the listening.

2. When it is your turn to talk, look the other person in the eyes, keep your comments short and to the point, and try to talk about something interesting to the other person.

3. When it is the other person's turn to talk, give your full attention and do not talk until the other person is finished.

4. If you did not hear something that has been said, say something like, "Excuse me, but I didn't hear what you just said. Could you please repeat it?"

5. If you did not understand something that has been said, say something like, "Excuse me, but I didn't understand what you just said. Could you please explain it?"

6. Whenever you talk with anyone, avoid bragging, exaggerating, lying, or trying to pretend that you know something you don't know. Doing these things may get you into trouble.

Ending a Conversation

You can end a conversation graciously by doing these two things:

1. Before you end a conversation, make sure the other person has had a chance to say all he or she wanted to say.

2. If you must end the conversation before the other person is finished talking, offer a sincere apology. Say something like, "I'm sorry that we cannot finish this conversation right now. Maybe we can finish it at another time."

Conversation Guidelines

There are things you can do to keep your conversation gracious.

1. Avoid using too many slang words, like *ain't, yep, nope, yeah, naw.* These words are offensive to many people.

2. Avoid whispering to someone in front of someone else. Whenever you whisper to one person in a group, you exclude everyone else in the group. This is unkind.

3. Avoid tattling (telling on someone).

4. Let every person tell his or her own story when ready
to do so.

5. Avoid criticizing other people and gossiping about them when they are not around. Don't say anything about other people that is untrue or unkind.

6. If you are upset or have a concern about another person, go directly to that person. Talk together and work it out.

Asking Questions

You can be gracious when you ask a question by remembering these two things:

1. Try not to ask questions that may hurt or embarrass anyone. Avoid asking about a person's personal affairs, finances, private thoughts and opinions.

2. Try not to ask questions that will force people into
   talking about something they do not want to talk about.

Answering Questions

You can be gracious whenever someone asks you a question by doing these three things:

1. When someone asks you a question you do not mind answering, give a clear, honest answer.

2. Whenever possible, explain your answer. That is, if your answer is yes or no, try to complete the thought, if you can do so easily.

3. When someone asks you a question you do not want to answer, do not ignore the question, or respond rudely by saying, "That's none of your business." Instead, say something like, "I'm sorry, but I would rather not answer that question at this time."

Whatever you ask or say to anyone, it will be well received if you do not ask or say anything that you would not want someone to ask or say to you. This is the most important thing to remember whenever you talk with someone else.

GRACIOUS RESPONSES

Giving Compliments

Whenever you give a compliment or a gift, you can be gracious by doing these things:

1. Be sincere. Do not say anything that you do not really feel or think is true. With regard to a gift, do not give anything you do not really want to give.

2. Look the people in the eyes while you are complimenting them or giving them a gift.

3. Say the compliment, or tell why you are giving the person the gift, clearly and loudly enough to be heard and understood.

4. Compliment a person as often as you can sincerely do so. You can never give a person too many compliments if the person genuinely deserves them.

Receiving Compliments and Gifts

You can receive compliments graciously by doing these things:

- Whenever someone gives you a compliment or gift, accept it without judgment and say thank you.

- Try not to refuse, deny, or put the compliment down in any way. Do the same with a gift.

- With regard to a gift, you may want to say, "It is kind of you to give me a gift."

- With regard to a compliment, you may want to say something like, "It is very kind of you to notice," or "It is very kind of you to say that."

Giving Apologies

Whenever you need to apologize, you can be gracious by doing several things:

1. Go to the person as soon as possible, look the person in the eyes, and admit that you were wrong. Never try to cover up your mistakes.

2. Sincerely say that you are sorry.

3. Ask the person to forgive you.

4. Do everything you can to make up for your wrongdoing. For example, if you broke another person's possession, try to replace it. If you said something bad about someone, go back to the person you talked to and straighten things out. Avoid making the same mistake again.

Accepting Apologies

Whenever someone apologizes to you, you can be gracious by doing several things:

1. Allow the person to explain the situation, saying all that needs to be said. When the person is finished, say, "I understand."

2. If the person says, "I'm sorry," accept the apology.

3. If the person asks forgiveness, forgive him or her.

4. If there is nothing the person can do about the mistake, say something like, "There is really nothing any of us can do. Let's forget the whole thing and go on from here."

5. If the person offers to do something to make up for the mistake, allow him or her to do it. Be sure to thank the person for what has been done.

Saying No

Whenever you must say no, you can be gracious by doing two things:

1. Say no kindly.

2. Whenever possible, give an honest explanation for why you have to say no.

Here are some kind ways to say no.

44

Saying Excuse Me

Saying excuse me is the gracious thing to do whenever—

- you must interrupt someone who is talking;

- you bump into someone;

- you interfere with something someone is doing;

- you say something that embarrasses or hurts someone. (In this case, you should follow your *excuse me* with *I'm sorry*.)

THE END of not knowing what you should say.